I'm the *Pretty* One,
You're the Smart One

I'm the Pretty One, You're the Smart One

515 Things Only Sisters Understand

Lorraine Bodger

**Andrews McMeel
Publishing**

Kansas City

06 07 08 09 10 WKT 10 9 8 7 6 5 4 3 2 1

ISBN-13: 978-0-7407-5717-4
ISBN-10: 0-7407-5717-2

Library of Congress Control Number: 2005932598

www.andrewsmcmeel.com

Illustrations by Lorraine Bodger
Book design by Holly Camerlinck

Introduction

There's no bond in the world like the bond between sisters. Just ask any sister of a sister, whether she's the oldest, the youngest, or anything in between. She may moan or groan or roll her eyes—but in the end she'll admit there's no one more important in her life than her sister. Parents are just parents, brothers are just brothers, best friends are just best friends, even husbands are just husbands, but sisters—well, sisters are the ones to whom sisters always turn in times of joy or trouble, celebration or crisis.

The closeness between sisters who have grown up together, even when there's a significant age spread, is a very special kind. You couldn't even begin to count the number of secrets you've told her, the number of secrets she's *guessed,* the number of midnight confidences you've shared. Who else knew what was going on behind the scenes of the day-to-day family drama? Only your sister. Who else knew where, when, and how you messed up or triumphed week in and week out? Only your sister. Who else knew, a heartbeat before you did, who your Mr. Right would be? Only your sister.

It's an intimacy born of years of common experience, an intimacy you can claim with no other person in your life. No one else has seen as many of your giggles, your rages, your sillinesses, your moments of bewilderment, or your vulnerabilities as your sister has. Your parents might not have noticed how upset you were about the French teacher who yelled at you or the hockey coach who tossed you out of the game, but your sister knew everything about it. Your brother wouldn't in a million years have cared whether you were battling with your fiancé, but your sister was on the case immediately. Your best friend might not have been aware of the brand-new tension between your parents, but your sister knew as much about it as you did. You and your sister sometimes—even often—disagreed about a lot of things, but you drew strength from each other, and that's what counted in the end.

Your sister's advice (solicited or unsolicited) carries weight. Her opinions matter. Her concern comforts you. Her encouragement keeps you going and her love keeps you centered. She's both a reflection of yourself and a totally different being, the standard against which you measure your progress and the standard against which you rebel. You don't want to be exactly like her—except sometimes. You see yourself the way she sees you—and wish you didn't. Her very presence can be a source of confusion—and yet she makes sense of the world for you.

You and your sister may decide to live your lives in opposite ways on opposite sides of the globe, but there will still always be a thousand similarities between you. Sometimes you think the two of you are like twins; at other times you think she's an alien from another planet. But you're in her orbit and she's in yours, and nothing can change that—nor would you want it to, if it came right down to making a choice. No matter how far apart you are in miles or years or mindset, you're always together as sisters. And there are some things only sisters understand.

How reassuring it is to know there's another *entire* wardrobe available . . . the minute your sister leaves the house.

That everything is more fun when you do it with your sister.

That you want to hold onto her so tightly
that she can never get away,
and at the same time you wish she'd disappear
so you could have a life completely your own.

Drawing a line down the middle of the bedroom.
You stayed on your side, she stayed on hers, and if anything
of hers happened to drift across to your side of the line—hooray!
It automatically belonged to you.

*H*ow to sweet-talk your way out of your sister's wrath when you've borrowed her

    a.   best cashmere sweater
    b.   car
    c.   diamond studs
    d.   favorite CD
    e.   credit card

once too often without her permission.

*W*hy the skirt you adored in the Hip-Hop Chicks Boutique
suddenly looks totally tacky, ugly, and uncool
the minute your sister flicks a glance over it and says,
"Why'd you buy *that* thing?"

*T*hat your mother *always* treated your sister better
than she treated you.

*T*hat your father was *always* easier on your sister
than he was on you.

*T*hat your parents *always* gave your sister
more presents than they gave you.

*T*he privilege of being the flower girl
at your older sister's wedding.

Exactly where you were when you didn't get in till 4 a.m.

*T*he agony of having to wear hand-me-downs,
especially hers.

Movies about sisters:

Hanging Up; Hannah and Her Sisters; Hush . . . Hush, Sweet Charlotte; My Sister Eileen; Having Our Say: The Delany Sisters' First 100 Years; The Lemon Sisters; Practical Magic.

𝒯hat getting revenge on your big sister
for her many crimes is sweeter than any candy, cookie, or
ice cream cone in the world.

𝒮he gives you the best Christmas presents of anyone.
She knows what you want almost before *you* do.

*W*hy she was the smart one and you were the pretty one.
Or vice versa.

*T*hat the NO TRESPASSING sign on your bedroom door meant
everyone, *especially* your sister.

*T*hat a NO TRESPASSING sign on *her* bedroom door
made it imperative for you to pound on that door
as loudly as you possibly could and keep pounding
until she opened it.

How glad you are that your sister blazed the trail for you
through school, but how hard it is for you to follow.

How much fun it was for you and your sister to
a. short-sheet your brother's bed
b. put salt in your brother's Wheaties
c. hide your brother's math homework
d. call your brother's girlfriend and tell her he told you
to tell her he's never going to speak to her again as
long as he lives
e. all of the above

Being allies in the War Against the Grown-ups.

Holding tightly to your sister's hand
when you were in any brand-new situation.

Arguing over who went first at the dentist.

Worrying about your parents worrying about your sister.

Playing School. Playing Store. Playing Hospital.

She was always telling you what you could and couldn't do.
Naturally, you retaliated by doing exactly the opposite,
regardless of whether it was what you wanted to do.

Secretly, you feel competitive with your sister.
Secretly, she feels just as competitive with you.

That you'll always be there for her and
she'll always be there for you.

How confusing it's been for you to understand
that you're the heroine of your own story, not your sister's.

Dragging out a story at the dinner table
so your parents would pay more attention to *you*
and less attention to your sister.

The pain of even temporary estrangement
after a big argument, even if you were right
and your sister was wrong.

*P*resenting a United Sisters Front against

a. the babysitter who wanted you to go to bed on time

b. the great-aunt who wanted you to act like little ladies

c. the neighbor who ratted on you about that broken window

d. the saleswoman who swore that the purple bathing suits with the hideous little skirts looked *gorgeous* on you

e. the school nurse who declared you couldn't possibly have identical stomachaches at identical moments

*T*he drama of running away from home—for a day.

𝒯hat getting stuck in traffic with your sister isn't lost time,
it's found time—for catching up, laughing, gossiping,
problem solving, and all the other things
you never have a moment for.

Sister Solidarity Forever.

𝒫utting a frog in your sister's bed and then waiting behind the
door to enjoy her shrieks when she climbs in.

*T*ricking your sister into doing something boring or hard
(like mowing the lawn or folding the clean towels) by desperately
begging your mom to please, please, please let you do it—
which guarantees that your sister will beg just as hard
for the privilege. Concede graciously.

*H*ow to convince your sister that
    a. Martians
    b. zombies
    c. vampires
    d. trolls
    e. goblins
are real, no kidding, cross your heart
and hope to die.

*C*rawling into bed with your sister because
you were terrified of the burglars you *knew* were waiting
to break into the house.

Wondering what happened to that close, close relationship
you and your sister had when you were kids.
Where did it go?

That she can tell you outrageous lies
and you'll *always* believe her.

That you can tell her outrageous lies
and she'll *never* believe you.

The essential daily phone call.

Being a sounding board for even the wackiest
of your sister's schemes.

*W*hy yours is the name your sister writes down
when the form asks for "next of kin."

*H*ow much you admire her.

*T*he conviction that the two of you
could hold off an army, if you did it together.

*W*hy she puts up with your silly moods:
Because you put up with hers.

*P*atiently combing the knots out of your younger sister's hair,
no matter how long it took.

How to tell your sister that
    a. the spaghetti is really white worms
    b. there's dog meat in her hamburger
    c. cheese is made from rotten milk
    d. a tree will grow in her stomach if she swallows an apple seed
    e. she'll die if she accidentally swallows her bubblegum

Giving each other chicken pox and measles.

Racing each other to the bathroom in the morning.

You and your sister both entered the same profession, and wow, is that fun. (Except when it's not.)

How you put her on a pedestal and then cried when she fell off. She felt terrible, too.

That even though you and your sister aren't twins, sometimes you feel like twins.

The ultimate squelch:
You're not my mother.
You can't tell me what to do.

Reminiscing over each ornament when you unpack the Christmas decorations and trim the tree. Only you and your sister remember every detail—the year she bought that stuffed Santa and the year you broke the little glass choo-choo train and the year the satin angel fell off the top of the tree . . .

Why you joined her sorority.

Why you didn't join her sorority.

$\mathcal{F}$eeling as if you've done a particular thing or been
to a particular place, only to realize that it wasn't *you* who had
done it or been there—it was actually your sister.

$\mathcal{W}$hose cat it really is.

$\mathcal{T}$he sad and sorry fact that you and your sister
just don't agree about the way to raise your children.

$\mathcal{B}$eing coached through ear piercing
by your already-pierced sister.

Exactly who has better
    a. legs
    b. breasts
    c. teeth
    d. eyes
    e. hair

Exactly who is better at
    a. math
    b. sports
    c. languages
    d. drawing
    e. singing on key

Exactly who is
    a. funnier
    b. sweeter
    c. smarter
    d. cuter
    e. nicer

Merge issues:

Sometimes you can't figure out where she ends and you begin.
Or you end and she begins.

The difference between a teeny-weeny argument
and a big fight. Why can't your parents understand this
as well as your sister does?

She taught you how to put on makeup.
And when to update it.

You taught her how to get the hair off her lip, legs,
underarms, and bikini line.

*H*ow terrified you were of the monsters under your bed.
Not to mention the ones hiding in the closet.

*H*ow much you hated the teachers who said,
"Why can't you be more like your sister?"

*Y*ou'll fight tooth and nail *with* your sister,
but you'll also fight tooth and nail *for* her.

Matching outfits. Matching haircuts. Matching Barbie dolls.

Where the last jelly doughnut disappeared to.

How hard it is to say no to your sister.

Older sisters rule!

She'll keep your darkest secrets, and you'll keep hers.
That's a promise.

The astonishing scope of your parents' unreasonableness.

The shocking scope of your parents' ignorance.

How to help your sister through
a. her first bout of cramps
b. her second pregnancy
c. her third marriage
d. menopause
e. all of the above

That if you died tomorrow, your sister would take care of your children as if they were her own. You'd do the same for her.

You'll hold her hand through all her trials and tribulations.

That your sister *always* snares the bigger piece of cake.
A law of nature.

Never to tease you when you've gained ten pounds,
on pain of death.

Whether you *really* had your period that day
when you begged off gym class.

*H*ow to survive a family Thanksgiving dinner
without losing your mind.

Books about sisters:

Little Women, by Louisa May Alcott; *Housekeeping*, by Marilynne
Robinson; *Pride and Prejudice*, by Jane Austen; *A Thousand Acres*, by
Jane Smiley; *Hons and Rebels*, by Jessica Mitford.

*T*hat you're a Peeping Tom, with an eye
to the window of your sister's life.

*T*hat she'll take care of you *again*
if you drink a little too much at a party and throw up
for half the night. But you'd *better not* make a habit of it.

*H*ow much you hated it when your mother sat you down and explained that you were going to have a baby sister. No way!

The right answers to the most important questions.

YOU: Do you think Mom loves you more than me?
YOUR SISTER: Of course not.

YOU: When you were my age did you have to be in bed by ten?
YOUR SISTER: Oh, no—by nine.

YOU: Do I look fat?
YOUR SISTER: Don't be idiotic.

YOU: Can I borrow twenty bucks?
YOUR SISTER: Anytime.

$\mathcal{P}$ouring the Coke into two glasses and putting the glasses side by side to make sure they were filled with precisely equal amounts.

The Sisters' Telephone Round Robin:

Sister #1 calls Sister #2 to tell her version of the latest family event, then Sister #3 calls Sister #2 to tell *her* version, then Sister #2 calls Sister #1 to update, then Sister #3 calls Sister #2 with some details she left out, then . . .

The Sisters' E-Mail Round Robin:

Same scenario, but with fewer words.

The obligation to point out to your sister that she's deluding herself about

    a.   her weight

    b.   her new hair color

    c.   the prospect of her new boyfriend getting serious

    d.   her possibilities for promotion at her job

    e.   writing the Great American Novel

Who was Daddy's girl and who was Mommy's.

Being mortal enemies—until one day
you discovered you're best friends.

Supporting women's rights because you have a sister.

*W*hy it was your sister's job to inform you that there is no Santa Claus, and no Tooth Fairy, either.

*H*aving a secret word that you could whisper to each other to bring on gales of laughter at any given moment.

The weird sense of taking emotional turns:

When your sister is up, you're down, and when you're up, she's down.

*L*eaving hideous sweat stains on her favorite silk blouse—
you know, the one she told you never, ever to borrow . . .

That parents are an organizing principle:

You and your sister can talk about them, laugh about them,
debate about them, problem-solve for them, tend to them,
and generally shape your relationship around them.

*H*aving intersecting networks of friends,
even when you're adults.

Being a good sport:

Your sister has to learn how to lose (to you, of course)
and not act like a baby about it.

The necessity to be nice to your sister's pooch even though he's old, smelly, and bad-tempered.

You both wanted to be
   a. great chefs
   b. Olympic divers
   c. explorers
   d. Picasso
   e. Aretha Franklin
Instead, you became who you are.

She wasn't allowed to touch *anything*—ANYTHING—
in your room.

How you can be obsessed with being the Younger Sister.

How you can be obsessed with being the Older Sister.

Complaining to your father about your sister.
Fat lot of good *that* did.

That an older sister's task in life
is to be responsible for her younger sister.

The dire consequences of calling her a goody-goody.

*W*ishing you could be one of the gang at your sister's pajama party, but having the bedroom door slammed in your face.

*H*earing a family story about your sister so many times that you think you were there when it happened— but it really happened before you were even born.

*Y*ou never minded when your sister got better SAT scores, won more tennis games, and had a cuter boyfriend. You never minded a bit. Sure you didn't.

*T*hat you don't appreciate her telling you that your new short hairdo makes you look butch. Unless that's what you were going for.

That if your mother gives your sister her big, beautiful, white china tureen, then she'd better give you something just as nice or there's going to be trouble. Big-time.

Running for class president because your sister was class president. Ditto for cheerleader, secretary of the French Club, vice president of the debating team, and managing editor of the school newspaper.

$\mathcal{T}$hrowing up on your sister's
    a.   social studies project
    b.   prom dress
    c.   bedspread
    d.   laptop
    e.   fiancé

$\mathcal{B}$eing sympathetic when your sister got a divorce
because you secretly loathed her husband.

$\mathcal{B}$eing deeply disappointed when your sister got a divorce
because you really liked her husband.

$\mathcal{F}$eeling so-o-o flattered when your younger sister comes to you
for advice, even when you know she's just buttering you up
before she asks to borrow something you don't want to lend.

$\mathcal{T}$rying hard to find a way to be adult friends,
now that childhood has been decisively left behind.

$\mathcal{S}$howing up in any kind of emergency, no matter how late
at night, how far away, or how scared you are.

$\mathcal{F}$eeling secure that you can have a career, take a break
to have a baby, and then go back to work,
because your sister has already done exactly that.

Right Brain Sister and Left Brain Sister:

She has the eye for wardrobe (hers *and* yours) and
interior decoration (ditto); you have the words
for term papers (yours *and* hers) and letter writing (ditto).

How much you hated it when your parents
held up your sister as an example.

She could handle day camp. You couldn't.

The time your first-grade teacher couldn't make you stop crying,
so she sent for your sister from the fourth-grade room.
You stopped crying the minute you saw her.

The family crisis that ensued when your sister accidentally spilled the beans about your impending
    a. elopement
    b. divorce
    c. career move to Hong Kong
    d. face lift
    e. remarriage

The family crisis that ensued when you took your sister's side about
    a. moving in with her boyfriend
    b. getting a motorcycle
    c. getting a nose ring
    d. becoming an organic farmer
    e. throwing her boyfriend out

Helping each other blow out the candles
on the birthday cake, yours or hers.

Going with your sister to buy a Christmas present for your mom—the first time you bought her a Christmas present with your own money.

That your favorite holiday is Thanksgiving, so it must be her favorite holiday, too, right? Wrong.

Pretending to sleepwalk—right into your sister's room.

Clapping louder than anyone else when your sister marched across the stage to accept her college diploma.

The sandbox, the seesaw, the slide, the jungle gym, and the swings at the playground.

Shared toys. Unshared toys.

*F*ighting over the best crayon colors.

*S*tarting a sentence that your sister finishes for you.

*S*neaking out of the house wearing wild and crazy outfits under your buttoned-to-the-chin coats.

*T*aking your sleeping bags out to the backyard on a velvety black summer night and watching the fireflies for hours.

*T*hinking your little sister is the absolutely most adorable thing in the universe.

The importance of teaching your younger sister
the art and craft of being a girl—how to

    a. hit the phone buttons without messing up those freshly
        polished nails
    b. blow dry to perfection
    c. buy underpants
    d. cry without melting her mascara
    e. ignore her appearance in favor of having fun

so you have the satisfaction of knowing that you passed
along your considerable female wisdom.

The importance of teaching your younger sister the basics
of home management—how to

    a. set the table
    b. empty the garbage
    c. fold the laundry
    d. load the dishwasher
    e. vacuum the living room

so you can supervise from the sidelines
while the chores get done properly.

The importance of teaching your younger sister the latest techniques in detective work—how to
  a. read a private letter by holding it up to the light
  b. eavesdrop on your parents
  c. pick the lock on a diary
  d. follow a boy without his knowing he's being followed
  e. pretend to be a grown-up on the telephone
so you can always be ten steps ahead of the game.

The importance of teaching your younger sister the fine points of haute cuisine—how to prepare
  a. grilled cheese-food sandwiches
  b. instant cocoa with marshmallows
  c. microwave popcorn
  d. slice-from-a-roll chocolate chip cookies
  e. chips and bottled salsa
so you won't starve to death.

The importance of teaching your younger sister the Tao of sports—how to

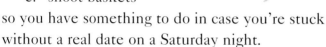

  a. play Go Fish
  b. play poker
  c. bowl
  d. shoot pool
  e. shoot baskets

so you have something to do in case you're stuck without a real date on a Saturday night.

The importance of teaching your younger sister the ways of the world—how to

  a. buy an airline ticket
  b. rent a car
  c. order from a menu in French
  d. figure out the tip
  e. use a credit card

so **you** never have to do the boring stuff when you go on a trip together.

The confusion between your own actual happiness and the notion that if you can make your sister happy, then you'll automatically be happy, whether you're really happy or not.

Having a better story (joke, complaint, excuse) than your sister in order to get your parents' attention.

Walking to school with your sister. Walking home for lunch with your sister. Walking back to school with your sister. Walking home after school with your sister.

How you gravitate to women who remind you of your sister and then end up treating them exactly the way you treat your sister.

Beach Games I:

Burying your sister up to the neck in sand and then leaving her there in the hot sun while you take a leisurely stroll along the boardwalk.

Beach Games II:

Chasing your sister up and down the beach, throwing jellyfish at her.

Beach Games III:

Stuffing *a lot* of sand down your sister's bathing suit.

*H*ow wonderful it is to see your sister sparkling, shining, and full of spirit, because it makes you feel better about yourself, too.

*H*ow sometimes you ignore your husband when your sister is around. She does the same thing.

*T*he encouraging e-mails she wrote to you in your first year of

    a.   college
    b.   living on your own
    c.   marriage
    d.   motherhood
    e.   widowhood

*H*ow cozy it was to read those nicely broken-in children's books that your sister loved and handed down to you.

Bonding over annoying your parents
from the back seat of the car.

Which of you got to make the rules
for the games you played together.

Being so angry at your kid sister that you bit her in the butt.

Making your sister laugh so hard in church that she
got sent out while you got to stay, looking angelic.

Performance pieces, also known as "putting on a show."
You played your clarinet, your sister did her recitation from
Edgar Allan Poe, you sang a duet ("Edelweiss" from
The Sound of Music or something from *Sesame Street*), and then
you wrapped up the show with a synchronized dance to
a hot cut from your mom's 1970's disco CD.

That when your sister confides in your husband about her love
affairs, it's just another form of flirting. Or worse.

Pushing, shoving, kicking, hitting, poking, punching,
and pinching for no reason at all.

Expert ridicule.

$\mathcal{G}$etting chubby together from eating too much fast food.

$\mathcal{C}$harging your sister exorbitant rates for emergency use of your

    a.   blow dryer

    b.   cell phone

    c.   history term paper

    d.   riding boots

    e.   dangly rhinestone earrings

*H*ow hard it's been for your older sister to let you grow up.
You'll always be younger, but you both know
you can't be her *little* sister forever.

*T*hat you and your sister are the only people on earth
who really understand your parents.

*T*he fear of the horrible illnesses that run in your family.

*H*ow hard it is to keep yourself in a positive
frame of mind when your sister is in a negative one.

How much you hated it when your Aunt Flora
gave you both exactly the same presents for Christmas,
but yours was blue and your sister's was red.

That you worshipped your sister for protecting you
from the bullies in the playground.

The fun of calling your sister from the top of the stairs—
and then bombarding her with pillows
when she appeared at the bottom.

The fun of hiding her favorite stuffed animal—
and then "finding" it for her.

The fun of telling her ghost stories so scary that she cried.

How crucial it was for you and your sister to buy lunch in the school cafeteria like the rest of the kids, even though the food was disgusting and your mom made perfectly good PB and J.

Dressing like your sister, without actually being aware you were doing it.

Being the first to
    a.   wear a bra
    b.   get grounded for staying out past curfew
    c.   flunk a class
    d.   bring a boyfriend home for dinner
    e.   have a fender bender

Well, *someone* had to be the first.

Turning on your favorite TV program and then sitting on the remote so your sister can't change the channel.

The solemn, full-scale funeral you held for the pussycat you got as a kitten and adored until her dying breath.

Treachery:

In the morning telling your sister a deep, dark secret—
and then hearing it all over school by noon.

Thinking that your new baby sister was your own
private, perfect, living doll.

Just saying no—to absolutely anything your sister
asked you to do, on principle.

Racing down to the living room together on Christmas morning.

Picking a huge bouquet of wildflowers for your mother.

*W*hat a relief it was to go into business with your sister because she's the only one you *really* trust with money.

*M*eeting her for a run each morning, knowing full well it's really meeting to talk and connect.

*T*he number of stories about your childhood you both remember—in completely different versions. How can that possibly be?

*T*he number of stories about your childhood you remember and she doesn't, and vice versa. Makes you wonder if you were living in the same house.

The maddening way your sister decides something about you
(for instance, that you're a picky eater) and sticks to it,
even in the face of overwhelming evidence to the contrary
(for instance, that you ate everything you were served,
including the oysters, the broccoli, the mushrooms,
and the revolting okra).

Feeling as if you grew up with two terrific mothers—
your real mom and your older sister.

The surprise you felt when you discovered that you
and your sister were *not* the same person.

Having exactly the same coloring.

Having exactly the same body type.

Having exactly the same funny-looking toes.

Making
   a. scrambled eggs
   b. spaghetti sauce
   c. guacamole
   d. BLTs
   e. mashed potatoes

exactly the same way as your sister.

Deciding you don't want kids because it was such a hard job taking care of your younger sisters for all those years.

Deciding you do want kids because it was so much fun taking care of your younger sisters for all those years.

*B*eing obligated to tell your dear darling sister
if something doesn't look good on her. A tough job,
but *someone* has to do it.

*H*aving to watch what you said because your sister would
pounce on anything boastful, boring, stupid, silly, inflated,
incorrect, mean, spiteful, untruthful, misleading, crazy,
or foolish that came out of your mouth.

*T*he sense of being on a shared journey, no matter how many
miles apart you and she might be.

*H*aving voices so similar that sometimes your parents couldn't
tell you apart when you answered them from another room.

*H*earing your sister's voice on her answering machine or voice mail and thinking it's your own voice.

*W*aiting, waiting, waiting for your sister to leave home (please, please, leave already!), and then missing her so much you could cry.

*H*ow to swear a blood oath of eternal enmity against your older siblings.

*W*anting your sister to think you're the coolest person in the galaxy.

Being generous:

Offering the last piece of liver to your beloved sister.

*T*eaching her to dance so you wouldn't look stupid
gyrating all over the living room by yourself.

*F*eeling as if you never got what you needed
because your sister could always yell louder for what *she* needed.

*S*neaking into your sister's room after lights-out to
    a. play gin rummy
    b. eat chocolate
    c. dish the dirt
    d. giggle
    e. all of the above
by flashlight.

*C*ompeting over who gave Mom the best present
on Mother's Day.

On her birthday, giving your sister a smack on the tush for every year of her life. How satisfying was *that?*

Waking your sister early in the morning to show her the first snowfall.

Nursing your mother through a long illness.

Nursing your sister through a long illness.

*G*roup rates on violin lessons, dancing lessons,
gymnastics classes, and tutoring.

*R*aking leaves, holding hands,
and jumping into the leaf pile like a pair of gazelles.

*T*he despair of being sister to a person
who knows exactly what to wear on every occasion
and never looks less than perfect.

*T*he fear that you'll make the same mistakes
your parents made.

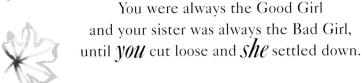

Role reversal:
You were always the Good Girl
and your sister was always the Bad Girl,
until *you* cut loose and *she* settled down.

Wait! Stop! There's a newborn sister in the house, but you haven't had enough time alone with your mommy and daddy yet! Send that baby back immediately!

Sitting on the floor, awestruck, watching your older sister get dressed for a big date. She was so beautiful and glamorous . . . and you were so gawky and grubby.

Basking in the warm glow of admiration from your silly little sister, while you dressed for a big date. She thought you were such hot stuff . . . she didn't know you were scared stiff.

*C*alling your sister on her birthday,
no matter where in the world she is.

*F*eeling competitive over her kids' and your kids' achievements.

The pleasure of cooking big family feasts together.

*O*n a bad day, thinking that if she weren't your sister
you wouldn't even want to know her.

*Y*ou're harder on her than you are on any of your friends.
But you let her off the hook sooner, too.

Telling your sister to
a. get over herself
b. get past it
c. get a grip
d. get a life
e. all of the above
knowing full well that you're doing it just to annoy her.

The family drama entitled "If You Girls Don't Stop
Fighting Back There We're Turning Around and
Going Right Home and I Don't Care How Disappointed
Grandma Will Be."

She got married first, and then you envied her cozy couples life.

She got married first, and then she envied
your independent single life.

It's amazing:

You're grown-ups now and you get along fine when you hang out together, but the minute you and your sister are in the presence of your parents you regress to childhood and revert to those bad old patterns of sisters behavior.

How hurt you'd be if your parents left everything to your sister's children, just because you didn't have kids.

Refusing to fight back against your sister, either verbally or physically. Why bother? She always won.

$\mathcal{W}$aiting for your sister (again)
  a. in the rain
  b. in a restaurant
  c. in front of her office building
  d. at the bus stop
  e. at the airport
and going berserk with impatience.

Being angry at your parents for telling your sister over and over
how pretty she was, even though everyone knew
you were actually prettier.

Convincing each other that the naughty, mischievous thing
you were about to do together was perfectly okay
and wouldn't get either of you into trouble.

Laughing so hard together that you both wet your pants.

Laughing so hard together that milk came out of your nose.

Being on the same team, psychically speaking.

*F*ollowing in your sister's footsteps.

*T*aking sides with one parent against the other.

Dividing up the chores according to ability:

You do anything that requires brains (like making a list of videos
the family might like to watch this week) and your sister does
anything that requires dumb strength (like everything else).

*K*nowing you don't have to be the best at absolutely everything.
You can leave a few things for your sister to be best at.

Emotional blackmail:

YOU, BRAVELY: That's okay, I can go to the prom in my sneakers, I know you needed those gorgeous black heels desperately and poor Mom couldn't afford to buy new shoes for both of us.

YOUR SISTER, WEARILY: Oh, for pity's sake, wear the wretched shoes to your prom!

More emotional blackmail:

YOU, SWEETLY: I'm so proud of you for losing all that weight and I understand perfectly why you'd want to reward yourself with that pint of Cookies 'n' Cream you just hid in the back of the freezer.

YOUR SISTER, QUICKLY: No, no, no, no, no, I bought it for you.

*T*hat it practically killed you when your sister left for college. The house was so-o-o-o empty without her.

❦

*T*hat it practically killed you when you had to leave for college because you knew your sister felt so abandoned.

❦

*T*he terrible silence at the dinner table when your parents were in the middle of a huge quarrel.

❦

*M*oving three thousand miles away to escape your family.

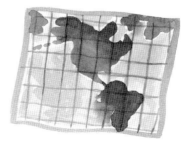

*T*hat your sister's house is your home-away-from-home.

*S*pending hours and hours and hours on the phone
with the coziest sister in the world.

Sisters who make (or made) music:
Alexa and Natalee, the Roches, the Simon Sisters, Sister Sledge,
the Lennon Sisters, the Boswell Sisters, the Andrews Sisters,
the McGuire Sisters.

*W*hy you sent her up the dark stairs first at bedtime:
Because you were such a scaredy-cat.

*M*aking remarks to your sister that are so insulting
you wouldn't *dare* to make them to anyone else.

*H*ow different two sisters from the same family can be. You're

a. shy and quiet
b. sensitive and easily hurt
c. steady and reliable
d. a one-woman support system for your family and close friends
e. a rule follower

*W*hile your sister is

a. noisy and full of laughter
b. bold and thick-skinned
c. intense and a little flighty
d. good buddy to dozens of pals
e. a rule breaker

Go figure.

Being stuck indoors on a rainy day, wailing "Mo-o-ommy, I have nothing to do!"

Whining.

Tantrums.

Interminable bickering.

*L*ifelong therapy.

*B*ragging about your sister's accomplishments as if she were your own kid.

Being a trio:

You, your sister, and your mom.

Children's books about sisters:

Sisters, by David McPhail; *The Twins*, by John Wallace;
The Mole Sisters series, by Roslyn Schwartz; *Venus and Serena
Williams: Grand Slam Sisters*, by Terri Morgan; *What Sisters Do Best*,
by Laura Numeroff; *The Five Sisters*, by Margaret Mahy; *Nancy and
Plum*, by Betty MacDonald; *I'm a Big Sister*, by Joanna Cole.

*Y*our sister opens up the world for you because
she likes to try new things, from food to music to hairstyles—
and if you want to spend time with her,
you have to try new things, too.

That if your sister is terrific at something,
you'll automatically go in the opposite direction
to avoid competing with her.

The importance of family food rituals, like meatloaf
every Monday, the IHOP on Sunday morning,
or ice cream sodas after shopping.

Which chat room you were *really* in when your mother
knocked on your bedroom door.

*I*f you're the married sister, you get to
  a. take care of your elderly mother while your unmarried sister gallivants all over the globe
  b. complain about your husband to your unmarried sister
  c. live in a house that's too small for you and the kids
  d. have empty nest syndrome, eventually
  e. feel as if all your clothes are out-of-date (which they probably are), stained with grape jelly (or worse), or don't fit (and never will again)

*I*f you're the unmarried sister, you get to
  a. take care of your elderly mother because your married sister has to take care of her family
  b. moan about your ghastly blind dates to your married sister
  c. live in an apartment that's too small for you and your roommates
  d. explain to your nieces and nephews why you don't have kids
  e. feel guilty for buying new clothes and apologize for them if you happen to bump into your married sister on the street

Secretly wishing your mother would step in and referee when you and your sister were having a fight.

Teaching your sister how to behave at a party.

Teaching your sister how to behave at an overnight.

The thrill of meeting your younger sister's plane when she comes for a visit.

How devastated you were when your parents split up.

That sisters' friendship is a friendship to fall back on when no one else is available.

That all hell could break loose when you have to divide up your mother's silver and china and jewelry.

That you'd never have survived your homesickness at sleepaway camp if your sister hadn't snuck into your bunk at night to give you a hug, or if you hadn't been able to take courage from her reassuring presence each morning at flag raising.

How your teenage sister could be
    a.   generous one minute and selfish the next
    b.   nice today and mean tomorrow
    c.   smiling at breakfast and sobbing at dinner
    d.   beautiful when she went on a date and a mess the next morning
    e.   all of the above

Hiding under the bed, in the cellar, behind a door, or in a closet when you've committed a crime against your sister and retribution is on the way.

That your sister is way out of line if she
flirts with your husband.

That she's asking for trouble if you call her on it
and she plays innocent.

That she's courting disaster if she doesn't stop.
Immediately and forever.

Having something bad happen to you—and being aced out
of the Sadness Olympics by your sister having
something worse happen to her.

Cinderella and her stepsisters. Snow White and Rose Red.

$\mathcal{M}$onopoly tournaments.

$\mathcal{P}$laying dress-up with your mom's old clothes on a rainy day.

$\mathcal{S}$pur-of-the-moment family outings.

$\mathcal{H}$ow much you loved it when your sister acted as emcee at your birthday parties.

The delight of coaxing a smile out of your new baby sister.

The joy of sharing a

    a. car
    b. stereo
    c. TV
    d. computer
    e. girlfriend

with your sister. Not.

That you often see the world through her eyes—and sometimes you wonder if she ever sees the world through yours.

That you know her intimately—but sometimes you wonder if you know her at all.

The silly songs you invented together.

The books you read together.

The piano lessons you hated together.

Hoping you'd get as many
   a. phone calls
   b. boyfriends
   c. valentines
   d. good grades
   e. party invitations
as your older sister. Never happened.

$\mathcal{W}$ho's like Mom and who's like Dad, and why.

$\mathcal{P}$arents who are never satisfied with anything you've accomplished.

$\mathcal{W}$ho was the official spokesperson for the two of you when you interacted with the grown-up world.

Shopping techniques:

You're a determined bargain hunter; your sister parts freely with her money. But over your years of shopping together you've become a little looser and she's developed a better eye for a deal. Works for both of you.

$\mathcal{H}$urrying downstairs to the dining room on birthday mornings to find presents stacked high at your place at the table.

Teaching your sister to swim when she was terrified of the water.
Now she's a lifeguard and you're proud of her.

The thrill of visiting your older sister at college.

Helping your sister dress on her wedding day.

Getting on (or staying off) the Mommy Track,
because your sister is already there.

Whom to call for help when you have to be
a. on a flight to the Hague to argue a case
   at the International Court of Justice
b. in emergency surgery
c. on your way to the client's office
   to make a career-changing presentation
d. at a press conference
e. accepting an award
and your child is throwing up every half hour.

Your mother's neurotic behavior.

Your father's neurotic behavior.

How comforting your sister was when you got your first period
and how proud you were to be as grown-up as she was.

*H*ow comforting your sister was when you lost your virginity.
Been there, done that. Survived.

*T*hat it's impossible for your older sister to understand
that you just don't want the same things she wants.

*T*hat it's impossible for your older sister to understand
that you're just not as brave as she is.

*W*ho had (and still has) the most common sense.

*T*hat the last person in the universe to notice
how much you've changed will be your sister.

𝒯hat you get sick and tired of her boyfriend angst,
and she gets sick and tired of your job angst.

Reality checks:

🌀 Hey, aren't those jeans a little tight?

🌀 Are you absolutely sure you want to wear your hair that way?

🌀 Can you actually get into a good school if your SAT scores are this low?

🌀 Did you know that there are eighty million single women in America and only ten million men?

🌀 Haven't you read that eating too many potato chips causes severe brain damage?

Why you pinched your newborn sister
and then pretended to comfort her when she cried.

That it was just an excess of love that made you hug
your new baby sister so hard that she screamed.

That you thought you'd be your sister's mentor forever
because you thought she'd *need* a mentor forever.

How adversity can bring the two of you together in an instant.

Being a private club of two.

When you were kids, holding hands and performing a song together at family gatherings.

Getting your fair share:

Watching like a hawk while your mother divided the last piece of pizza in half with mathematical precision, so you were sure your sister didn't get a bigger piece than you did.

Why you needed to leave home.
Why you needed to come back.

$\mathscr{F}$lirting with your sister's boyfriend when you were only
   nine: You teased.
   thirteen: You tested.
   seventeen: You transgressed.
   twenty-one: You were totally inappropriate.
Now—to your sister's relief—you've got your own boyfriend.

$\mathscr{A}$ccusing your sister of being disgustingly negative
about everything.

$\mathscr{A}$ccusing your sister of being disgustingly positive
about everything.

$\mathscr{F}$ighting over who gets to use the telephone first,
and for how long.

Giving your sister a new hairdo.

*T*reating yourselves to a spa weekend together
so you can catch up on everything.

*T*hat nobody can hurt you like your sister can hurt you.

*G*oing abroad together in search of your ancestral roots.

Sisters' Law I:

Just because you do everything right
doesn't mean your parents will love you more.

Sisters' Law II:

Just because you do everything wrong
doesn't mean your parents will love you less.

Deciding you'll never make the same mistakes your sister made,
and then making them anyway.

Forming a We Hate Brothers Club.

Undershirts.

Twin beds.

*R*ites of passage.

❦

*T*he fear that someone will find out your terrible family secrets.

❦

*S*ometimes you get *really, really* tired of being her younger sister.

❦

*S*ometimes she gets *really, really* sick of being your older sister.

❦

*I*gnoring your sister's warnings against investing in

    a. dot-coms
    b. imported unpasteurized cheese
    c. a revolutionary kind of dog food
    d. Fat Busters, Inc.
    e. all of the above

and regretting it for the next fifty years.

Early business training
you undertook together:

babysitting, throwing kids' birthday parties, gardening,
raking leaves, running errands, taking care of kids after school,
baking cookies, selling lemonade, walking dogs.

Fighting the important political battles, like when you
had to get up on Saturday morning (not late enough!),
when you could wear lipstick (not soon enough!),
and when you could get a tattoo (never!).

*I*nventing the meanest, nastiest nickname you can think of for your mean, nasty sister, and never missing an opportunity to use it.

*W*ishing your younger sister would go home to somebody else's house every now and then.

*T*hat you fought fiercely to protect her from the bullies in the playground. And bragged about it *forever*.

*T*hat you must never, never snitch out your sister.

*T*hinking you know what's going on inside your sister's head— and being shocked when you find out you don't.

*T*hat your older sister was your very first teacher,
long before you went to kindergarten.

abcdefgh 1+2+3=6

*B*eing furious at your sister for her refusal to acknowledge
what dreadful people your parents were.

*B*eing furious at your sister for her refusal
to see how insane your parents were.

*K*eeping your mouth absolutely shut when you had that
brief affair with a married man, because your sister was
married and she would have totally freaked out.

$\mathcal{F}$eeling as if there wasn't enough of your parents' love
to go around.

$\mathcal{F}$eeling as if your parents pitted you and your sister
against each other.

$\mathcal{F}$eeling as if you'll never be the one to do anything new because
whatever you think of, your sister has already done it.

$\mathcal{G}$etting in trouble together by
   a. burying a dead bird in the backyard, in your mother's
       velvet-lined jewelry box
   b. reading your parents' sex manuals
   c. skipping out on your chores in favor of the movies
   d. stuffing yourselves with too much Halloween candy
   e. forgetting to feed the puppy even though you swore you'd
       take turns doing it

How sad it is to realize that there are some things
the two of you will never agree on.

How comforting it is to realize that there are so many things
the two of you will *always* agree on.

That most of the time (all of the time?) your sister
just wouldn't listen to you,
even though you were giving her the best possible advice.

Disapproving of the way your sister raises her kids—
and feeling guilty for feeling disapproval.

The joy of having a sister living in a faraway place,
so you can take a vacation there.

Coveting your sister's piggy bank.

Coveting your sister's savings account.

That over time, the age difference between you and your sister matters less and less.

Remembering to tell your sister the bad news. Forgetting to tell her the good news.

The incredible deliciousness of your mother's homemade
  a. biscuits
  b. chicken soup
  c. Christmas cookies
  d. mac and cheese
  e. enchiladas

How mad it made you when your sister and her girlfriends hid from you. Made you lonely, too.

Arguing about who got to wear which costume on Halloween. Why did *she* always get to be the princess?

Freedom of choice meant freely choosing to do whatever your sister told you to do or she'd sock you on the arm.

*M*aking place cards for Thanksgiving dinner together.

*M*aking your Christmas list the easy way:
You wanted what she wanted.

Dyeing Easter eggs together.

*T*he sound of your mother's exasperated voice calling,
"Girls! Stop it!"

*T*he sound of your mother's sweet voice whispering,
"Good night, girls, sleep tight."

*H*ow much you hated leaving your friends and moving to a new state. Your sister hated it just as much.

*H*ow threatening it feels to be confronted by your sister over your
    a.   weight
    b.   emotional insecurity
    c.   financial insecurity
    d.   lack of a mate
    e.   all of the above

*C*lothes shopping with your sister and knowing her taste so well that you bring exactly the right things back to her in the dressing room without being told what she wants.

*Y*ou'll keep in touch with her any way you can.
By phone, letter, e-mail, carrier pigeon—whatever it takes.

*T*hat sometimes when you disagree with your sister
it's just plain smarter to keep silent than to risk a fight.

That you can be good friends but not best friends.

*T*hat your sister drives you crazy and you drive her equally crazy.

*E*ven though she pulled your hair, she didn't mean it.

*E*ven though you pinched her arm, you didn't mean it either.

You will always race to the phone to tell your sister about a new

    a.   man

    b.   job

    c.   hair stylist

    d.   diet

    e.   gynecologist

The sneaky satisfaction of being the first to get married.

Coveting your sister's clothes and being overjoyed
when she finally gets tired of them and gives them to you.

That you'll *never* tell your sister the real story
about your sex life.

That she's the *only* one you'd tell the real story
about your sex life.

Family vacations on which nothing went right
(and you know whose fault *that* was).

The first funeral you ever went to.
Thank heavens your sister was there with you.

Feeling as if it's a miracle when you and your sister
get along for more than five minutes at a time.

*Y*ou hated babysitting your younger sister,
even when your parents paid you to do it.
Didn't they know you'd rather be out with your friends?

*Y*ou resented the fact that your parents had to *pay*
your older sister to babysit you. Didn't she *like* staying home
with you when everyone else went out for the evening?

*P*lanning the annual family reunion together.
What a relief that she's the world's most organized human being.

*G*oing with your sister's husband to buy her a piece of jewelry because only you know exactly what she'd want.

*T*elling your sister some truly awful things about your husband— and wishing, an hour later, that you'd kept your big mouth shut.

*H*ow shaky you were on the first day of your first job. The pep talk your sister gave you got you through the day.

*A*cting really crazy so no one would think you were anything like your big sister, Miss Perfect.

*T*eaching her how to use the self-service fill-'er-up thingy at the gas station.

The fear that your friends will make fun of your mother because she
  a. doesn't speak English very well
  b. insists you attend Sunday School
  c. works all the time and can't go to PTA meetings
  d. left your father
  e. dresses too young for her age

The fear that your friends will make fun of your father because he
  a. comes from another country
  b. works two jobs and is never around
  c. jokes with your friends and sounds like a dork
  d. rules the house as if he were king
  e. isn't interested in the stuff other fathers are interested in, like football and baseball

Being a pest.

Reading your sister's diary.

Being jealous of her passionate love affairs.

When your older sister got married,
you were glad to get rid of her.

When your older sister got married,
you couldn't believe she was leaving *you* for *him*.

Staying up together to watch the Academy Awards.

Staying up together to watch the ball drop
on New Year's Eve.

That your husband had better not say anything sarcastic
about your sister or he'll be sorry.

That your sister is your go-to person.

That a friend may disappear, but a sister is forever. Help!

That you and your sister always felt like partners in crime.

When it comes to the crunch, you won't do anything
that will upset her permanently.

How surprised you were when your parents explained
that your new baby sister wasn't actually *your* baby at all.

The dear little round plastic wading pool you
and your sister splashed in when you were tots.

The excitement of Family-Christmas-Tree-Buying Day.

$\mathcal{T}$he pleasure of
- a. having a double wedding
- b. moving next door to each other
- c. getting pregnant at the same time
- d. raising your kids in tandem
- e. all of the above

$\mathcal{H}$ow much you loved the Girl Scouts. (She did, too.)

$\mathcal{H}$ow much you hated the Girl Scouts. (She did, too.)

How to tolerate her gerbil (hamster, white mouse, iguana).

Prolonged name calling. A contest of true intellect and wit, a test of vocabulary, a mind game worthy of Mr. Spock.

Fighting over who got to watch what when on TV.

That you must never bad-mouth your sister to her children, no matter how angry she's made you.

*D*espairing because you're sure your sister's grandchildren are so much better behaved and so much smarter than your own grandchildren.

*B*eing a spy, a detective, an undercover agent in order to find out what your sister was up to.

*T*hat you must never criticize your sister to her face, if you know what's good for you.

*M*aking a mad dash for safety—your sister's house— when the hurricane hit.

That when your little sister was born
you were sure your parents were going to give you away.

The unreasonable things your mother insisted on:
    a.   baths
    b.   meals
    c.   school
    d.   sleep
    e.   thank-you notes

Kicking each other under the table
while keeping straight faces above it.

Who *ought* to sit in the front seat:
You, because you get carsick.

Who actually gets to sit in the front seat:
Your older sister, because she pulls rank.

Being irritated with your sister's obsessive dieting.

That certain Sister Dynamics never change,
no matter how old you get.

Pool Games I:

Challenging your sister to a race—one, two, three, GO!—
and then staying right where you are while she swims
like a demon for about three laps before she realizes
you were putting her on.

Pool Games II:

Pretending to drown, and scaring the living daylights
out of your sister.

Pool Games III:

Diving beneath your sister and pulling her legs out
from under her. Ten times in a row.

Making her go with you when you have to discuss something heavy-duty with your parents, on the (sometimes mistaken) assumption that she'll take your side.

How endlessly you and your sister compare notes on *everything*.

Trailing your sister like a faithful puppy dog.

Having the same last name.

The teacher calling you by your sister's first name.

Doing something—*anything*—for the sole purpose of being different from your sister.

$\mathscr{P}$roviding a diversion when your parents brought up an unwelcome topic (like who on earth could have taken a nip from the bottle of brandied pears or who's been making calls to Argentina).

$\mathscr{T}$he day the

a. squirrel
b. pigeon
c. raccoon
d. swarm of bees
e. neighbor's Doberman

got into the house and chased you and your sister from pillar to post.

$\mathscr{F}$eeling terribly, terribly vulnerable when your sister criticized you.

*W*aiting (and waiting and waiting) for your sister to
GET OFF THE PHONE!

*T*aking a little joyride in your mom's car—
before either of you had a license.

Dermatology:
She's an expert on zits. *Your* zits.

*H*aving matching migraines.

*H*opping in the car and hitting the open road
for the entire summer.

The fear that your marriage will turn out as badly
as your parents' marriage.

The fear that your marriage won't turn out as well
as your parents' marriage.

Being glad your sister shared a bedroom with you
because you'd be lonely without company.

Hating to share a bedroom with your sister
because you never had a moment of privacy.

The absolute necessity for sensible emotional boundaries.
Good luck with that one.

𝒯aking your sister to her first
    a.   rock concert
    b.   sorority meeting
    c.   dance club
    d.   Lamaze class
    e.   all of the above

𝒯rading Christmas presents when you got the striped sweater she wanted and she got the suede gloves you wanted.

𝒲ho was (and still is) the bossiest sister in the universe.

*W*ho they were thinking of when they invented
the word "controlling."

*W*hose picture is in the dictionary,
right beside the definition of "pain in the neck."

*B*eing wildly jealous of the great parties your sister throws
and being desperately grateful that she condescends
to invite you at all.

*H*aving a partner to help make those critical decisions
about your aging parents.

*H*aving a buddy when you go to visit your aging parents
in a nursing home or hospital.

$\mathcal{T}$humbing through the family albums together
for hours and hours at a time.

$\mathcal{E}$ating the weird food your sister made
when it was her night to cook for the family
and telling her it was delicious. Or not.

$\mathcal{B}$eing sent to your room to cool off.

$\mathcal{B}$eing sent to your room as punishment.

The rules about after-school snacks.

Clinging to your sister for dear life during scary movies or videos.

Merciless teasing.

Merciless tickling.

How maddening it was when you temporarily lost her to her Grand Passion for

    a. horses

    b. soccer

    c. the rain forest

    d. the boys on the fencing team

    e. the Dixie Chicks

Summer days were more fun
because she was there to share them.

She explained sex to you before your mother did.

Becoming the confidante of your sister's teenage daughter,
a secret arrangement worked out between you and your sister
so she could be sure her daughter had a reliable adult to turn to.

You and your sister have the same sense of humor. You can keep each other laughing for hours on end.

That little bit of disappointment you feel when your sister tells her Big Secret to her best friend instead of telling it to you.

That if you have a tight relationship with your sister, you either *never* look for sister substitutes among your friends, or you *always* seek out friends who become as close to you as sisters.

How nice it is that she loves your husband like a baby brother, as long as she doesn't try to change his diapers.

Unsolicited advice on a range of topics from
how to make salad dressing to how to write a résumé
to how to have a baby to how to stencil the living room walls.

The Litmus Test:
Worrying about whether your sister
will like your new boyfriend.

Painting your baby sister's teeny-weeny toenails.

Cutting your sister's bangs too short. Uh-oh.

*Y*es, I can. No, you can't. Yes, I can. No, you can't.
Can. Can't. Can. Can't. (Burst into tears.)

*M*oral support—
unquestioning, undying, unexpected.

*D*ashing outside together
to make the first snow angels.

*T*aking you down a peg.

*B*uilding you up a mile.

$\mathcal{T}$hat when you finally locate the very best
    a. cupcake
    b. pool hall
    c. moisturizer
    d. antique store
    e. bargain in fluffy terry towels
it is imperative that you share the information with your sister immediately.

$\mathcal{P}$leading your sister's case for getting a dog, so that she'd plead your case for a trip to Disneyland.

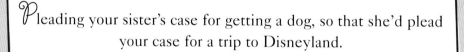

$\mathcal{P}$ressing your ear to your sister's bedroom door
to hear the secrets she and her girlfriends were telling.

$\mathscr{P}$retending you're going to let your sister ride your new bike
and then *at the last second*
grabbing it from her and riding away as fast as you can.

$\mathscr{P}$retending you're going to share the last cookie
with your sister and then *at the last second*
stuffing the whole thing into your mouth.

$\mathscr{P}$retending you're finally handing over the GameBoy
and then *at the last second*
snatching it back and hiding it.

$\mathscr{T}$hat instead of running home to Mom and Dad
when you're in transition, you can take refuge at your sister's.

The unmitigated pleasure of being an aunt
to your beloved sister's children.

That there's no detail of daily life too insignificant
for discussion.

Always knowing where your sister is.

Why you plan to live together when you're both widows.

How easily your sister can read your mind.

How much you trust her.

How much you depend on her.

How much you love her.